The Bluffer's Guide to
The Simpsons

Paul Couch

Oval Books

Published by Oval Books
335 Kennington Road
London SE11 4QE
United Kingdom

Telephone: +44 (0)20 7193 1769
E-mail: info@ovalbooks.com
Web site: ovalbooks.com

Series Editor – Anne Tauté

Cover designer – Vicki Towers
Cover image – © Douglas Kirkland/Corbis
Printer – J H Haynes & Co Ltd
Producer – Oval Projects Ltd

Cover: Matt Groening with The Simpsons

The Bluffer's® Guides series is based
on an original idea by Peter Wolfe.

The Bluffer's Guide®, The Bluffer's Guides®,
Bluffer's®, and Bluff Your Way® are
Registered Trademarks.

ISBN-13: 978-1-906042-06-6
ISBN-10: 1-906042-06-3

CONTENTS

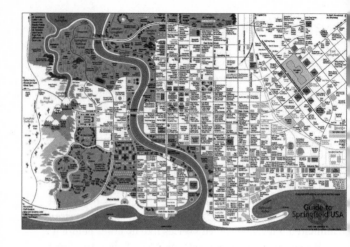

THE SIMPSONS' HOME TOWN

Bluffers should gratefully acknowledge those true aficionados who help us bring *The Simpsons* to life by embellishing their world with such detailed material as the map of the Simpsons' home town of Springfield that we show here.

So complex is the backstory of this fictional animated family that entire neighbourhoods and separate towns now exist in which their adventures may be broadened.

Of course, this map is not shown to be read, but rather to give bluffers an idea of the scale of the Simpsons' world. A detailed version may be procured from www.mapofspringfield.com, where the exquisite labours of Jerry Lermer and Terry Hogan can be examined in all its glory.

Before long, bluffers will find themselves effortlessly able to give directions to the Dalai Lama Expressway.

INTRODUCTION – HOMER WHO?

Bluffing your way in *The Simpsons* probably sounds more difficult than it actually is. After all, this global phenomenon has hundreds of characters and an equal number of sub-plots – we're not talking about Bugs Bunny here. The minutiae in which the stable of respected television writers saturate each episode might appear daunting. But, with a little patience, the dedicated and experienced enthusiast will be more than up to the task.

Let's start, as they say, from the ground up...

The Simpsons, created by a genius called Matt Groening (pronounced 'Groaning'), is an American animated television comedy series like no other before it.

It's set in the fictional town of Springfield – the exact location of which on the North American continent is never divulged – and revolves around the lives, loves and often unlikely adventures of a typical middle-class American family. Not the palatable, saccharine-coated mush that Brits have come to expect from over the Pond, though, oh no – *The Simpsons* is a warts-and-all depiction of how a real family interacts, magnified a hundredfold. The only difference is that the characters are predominently banana-yellow of complexion and have only four digits on each hand (except God, who has five, but that's a topic for the Advanced Bluffer that we'll tackle later on).

So detailed is the backstory of *The Simpsons* that we know that one Simpson child is violently allergic to seafood, that a peripheral character has had a heart bypass operation, and that several others have issues with alcohol dependency and eating disorders. Try that collar on for size, Scooby Doo...

After more than two decades on the small screen, The Simpsons boasts the honour of being the longest-running

American sitcom and the longest running American animated programme. Sometimes the stories are fairly straightforward – beginning, middle and end – sometimes they're just downright bizarre.

Happily, you needn't worry about these nuances. Successfully bluffing one's way in *The Simpsons* is simply a matter of arming oneself to the teeth with a few fundamental facts, keeping a sneaky arsenal of staggeringly obscure trivia stuffed down one's socks for emergencies, and brazening it out. Try it. The sense of smug superiority as you casually toss into conversation the fact that all three post-Lennon Beatles appeared in the series as themselves, or that Michael Jackson once used an alias to play a character pretending to be Michael Jackson, is pretty satisfying.

SIMPSONS BLUFFER'S RULE #1

The Simpsons is never, ever, referred to by the bluffer as 'a cartoon'. It's incredibly high-quality animation produced by a stable of respected, and highly paid, writers and animators. When you explain this sagely to your bluffee(s), it is appropriate to do so with the sort of almost imperceptible sneer usually reserved for those who admit to trainspotting.

Tell them with a cocky flourish that the Simpsons phenomenon has evolved entire backstories and an extended family of hundreds of characters that *The Flintstones* at the height of their popularity could only ever have dreamed rocky dreams about.

In later chapters, we'll look at the multitude of characters in more detail, take a tour around Springfield itself, deconstruct some classic episodes and, of course, learn those must-have catchphrases, but all that would be pointless without some idea, of where it all began.

D'oh! An Idea...

Imagine you wanted to create a cultural icon that would make you rich beyond the dream of avarice. Well, like all successful formulas, you'd probably start with something that would be instantly recognisable to your audience's personal experience. In this case, well-meaning, blue-collared oaf Homer Simpson and his progeny, the 10-year-old tearaway, Bart. Once you have the core concept, the rest is just sophisticated window dressing.

But a storyline that centred purely upon this father-son dynamic would probably run out of steam fairly quickly, so throw into the mix Homer's long-suffering wife, Marge, and daughters Lisa and baby Maggie for good measure. Then things start to take off – more by fluke than design – and your product goes from being functional to ever more sophisticated.

Homer gets a father of his own and an odd-though-likeable group of cronies; Marge's character expands too, as does those of their three children. Their house becomes a street called Evergreen Terrace, the street becomes a town called Springfield and, before you can say 'cash cow', the entire concept is snowballing towards a multi-billion dollar franchise.

There you have it – the makings of a global phenomenon and all that the aspiring cartoonist Matt Groening had to do back in 1987 was to pitch his idea to the Suits at Fox Television and watch as the money rolled in.

It all sounds like the American Dream. But bluffers will remind listeners that real life isn't that convenient. Down in the lobby of the Fox building, summoned for a meeting with producer James L. Brooks, the 35-year-old Groening had no intention of pitching *The Simpsons*. He'd never even heard of *The Simpsons*. They were a happy accident brought about by blind panic. The real reason he was there was to talk about a comic book strip he'd been working on called *Life in Hell*. Then, in a moment of clarity fuelled by fear and adrenaline, Groening realised that he'd probably lose all commercial rights to the work, which he'd nurtured since the 1970s and very much considered to be 'his baby'.

In desperation, and with the meeting fast approaching, he grabbed a scrap of paper, and there in the foyer, cobbled together a new idea.

Groening's own parents were called Homer and Margaret, so no brilliant creativity required there. Real-life sisters Lisa and Maggie came next, and Bart was modelled on a grotesque version of Groening himself as a child , 'Bart' simply being an anagram of 'Brat'.

They needed a home. *The Simpsons*' Springfield doesn't exist but the name is one of the most common for towns in the USA so Groening simply plucked it out of thin air as their base of operations.

Fifteen minutes to create television history and Matt Groening didn't even have to break into a sweat.

Ker-ching!

Eat My Shorts

Jim Brooks was suitably impressed with Groening's very crude sketches of *The Simpsons* and invited him to write some 60-second animated skits called 'bumpers' to be featured in a new project he'd been working on, *The*

Tracey Ullman Show.

Tracey Ullman had already been making waves in America for a number of years. Previously, the English comedienne Ullman had joined Red Nose Day front-man Lenny Henry and The Bloke Who's Name No-one Can Ever Remember in a BBC sketch show called *Three of a Kind*. Seeking fame and fortune, Ullman moved to the US and made squillions clowning around in a cod-Cockney accent, which our Colonial cousins naturally lapped up like hickory smoke barbecue sauce.

Not that the two comics left behind were in anyway bitter. Oh no.

Nobody could have ever imagined that the throwaway *Simpsons* segments would gain a cult following that would eventually eclipse the show that spawned them. Brooks' idea was that the embryonic Simpsons would feature in these daft little cameos before and after each commercial break. They weren't even complete stories, merely two-dimensional snapshots with a usually surreal slant.

For Groening, however, they were a very lucrative Frankenstein's Monster waiting to be unleashed.

While Ullman subsequently appeared in *The Simpsons* episode *Bart's Dog Gets an F*, relationships have not always been so rosy. In 1992, she brought a legal action against 20th Century Fox, demanding a $2.5 million slice of the pie when the Springfield-fest became a surprise runaway hit. "I breast-fed those little devils", she famously announced. Evidently the LA Superior Court was not impressed with her maternal skills and Ullman got nothing...nada...zilch. But don't be too disappointed for her – at one point Ullman's wealth was estimated at around £75 million, so she won't be going short of a Simpsons branded chocolate bar or two anytime soon.

There's No Face Like Homer...

So, you wander over to your local wildlife park, drag some ape out of his tree, stuck a crayon into his hairy mitt and ask him to draw *The Simpsons*. After he's finished jumping on your head, he'd probably give back something resembling Groening's initial drafts. The Simpsons we will get to know and love today bore little resemblance to early sketches; the renderings were chaotic to say the least and the animation jerky – almost eastern European in its simplicity.

The problem was that, when Groening handed his drawings over to the animators, he not unreasonably expected them to use the roughs as a basis for something far slicker. Instead, the finest artistic minds of the Klasky Csupso animation house simply traced over them. And that's what you get for employing company with a name that sounds like a Polish table sauce.

You gotta have talent

While voiced today by the same actors as at the start, Homer and family even sounded different in the early days. Compare a wax cylinder recording to a modern CD and you'll get the idea.

Homer fell to jobbing actor Dan Castellaneta who had the Ullman-era character sounding much smarter and more laid back than he does today, an unnatural progeny of Jack Lemmon and Disney's Goofy, if you will. In fact, Homer's voice was based on that of Castellanetta's own father.

Julie Kavner's Marge, however, was quieter and more stupid sounding than the modern one. Oh and her trademark hair-do was far smaller.

Spiky-haired Lisa was given to French-born, American-raised actress Yeardley Smith, whose vocalisation has probably stayed much the same, while the challenge that is Bart Simpson went to long-time voice talent Nancy Cartwright. Just about everyone in the cast has voiced baby Maggie at some point, as the main requirement seems to be to suck a dummy convincingly and gurgle on cue. Nice work if you can get it.

On December 17, 1989, and after three and a half seasons as 60-second 'bumpers' on *The Tracey Ullman Show*, The Simpsons finally hit the small screen as a series in its own right with the first season of 20-minute full-length stories.

The rest, as they say, is history.

SIMPSONS BLUFFER'S RULE # 2

The competent bluffer should always refer to the performers who play The Simpsons as 'the voice talent' never 'actors'.

For extra effect, drop their first names and simply use 'Castellaneta' (Homer), 'Kavnar' (Marge), 'Mantegna' (Fat Tony) and so forth. This implies some tacit familiarity and your bluffee will simply melt before your eyes like the witch in the *Wizard of Oz*.

MELLOW YELLOW – THE MAIN PLAYERS

The Simpsons are without doubt the First Family of Springfield. The others don't even make the A-list. You can't even begin to be a master of *Simpsons* lore without memorising the following details, so pour yourself a cool, malty Duff (oh yeah!) while enjoying a slab of Marge's Friday night meatloaf, and memorise the following as though your life (well social life, anyway) depended on it. It probably does.

Homer J. Simpson

Always on the brink of 39 years old, extraordinarily fat and stupid but with a heart of gold to match his skin pigment (if you could find it through all the blubber). Homer had a wonderful head of brown hair until about...er... 10 years ago (see: Bart)

Homer's hobbies comprise eating, sleeping, and drinking at Moe's – in that order. Frankly, it's a bit of a toss-up whether Homer loves his dysfunctional family or his bar-room cronies more but the family probably wins by a gnat's nose. If he could eat, sleep and spend quality family time at Moe's, Homer would reach his own particular nirvana.

Homer has a job in Sector 7-G at Springfield Nuclear Power Plant as a Safety Supervisor. However, for an intellectual lightweight with few academic, athletic, social, or any other discernable skills for that matter, Homer has had plenty of other callings over the years, including astronaut, CEO, farmer, food critic, teacher, author, heavyweight boxer, Country Music manager and circus freak. He's failed miserably at all of them.

He is famed for getting into all kinds of scrapes and, by way of a series of logic-defying strokes of luck, getting to travel all over the world. But fate has Homer's feet nailed very firmly in Springfield, where he invariably returns.

Homer's marriage to Marge has been occasionally rocky but always sound. You can't really imagine Fred and Wilma Flintstone making the same kind of amorous noises in the boudoir (and several other locations over the years) but the Springfield Posh & Becks seem to have no qualms about getting jiggy with it after lights out and, occasionally, with the lights on.

Killer trivia: Homer's email address is: chunkylover53@aol.com.

Marjorie 'Marge' Bouvier-Simpson

Nobody has ever satisfactorily explained away Marge's trademark beehive, the height of which is as impressive as its deep blue hue. So, let's do some reckoning: If Marge is the average height for a woman – say 165cm – then her barnet has to be in excess of 140cm. Add those together and Mighty Marge Simpson stands over 10 feet tall in old money.

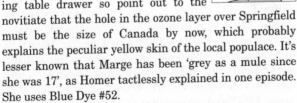

It's known that Marge keeps a couple of dozen cans of hairspray in her dressing table drawer so point out to the novitiate that the hole in the ozone layer over Springfield must be the size of Canada by now, which probably explains the peculiar yellow skin of the local populace. It's lesser known that Marge has been 'grey as a mule since she was 17', as Homer tactlessly explained in one episode. She uses Blue Dye #52.

Marge is the glue that holds the Simpsons together. Without her constant cleaning, scrubbing, mopping, and gentle nagging, this ever dysfunctional family would implode. Marge is always there to provide Homer's damage limitation, defend her son, rally along her eldest daughter, or just keep the baby happy. Marge's many duties often go unnoticed but, on occasion, she has been known to take up a cause or job and stick to it through the end. Examples of this include her stand against cartoon violence, her brief stint as a real estate agent, and her short-lived career as a cop.

Marge can always be trusted upon to make the most ethical of decisions. While she sometimes slips into the background – and occasionally into prison (for doing the wrong things for all the right reasons) – Marge is still an ever-present force in the *Simpsons* world, ready to catapult into the spotlight whenever she is needed and provide an alibi for her nearest and dearest.

Killer trivia: Marge was in labour for 53 hours before giving birth to Bart.

Bartholomew 'Bart' Jo-Jo Simpson a.k.a. **The Boy, El Barto, Bartman**

"Underachiever and proud of it!" Remember those omnipresent T-shirts? They're the ones that kicked up a stink in the late 1980s and the source of the kerfuffle was, as usual, Bart Simpson. The heady mixture of fear and admiration that Bart engendered in Springfield is paralleled in Our World where some conservative parents have blocked access to the character by their offspring who hail him as a role model.

In 1998, *Time* magazine rated Bart Simpson as

Number 48 in the Top 100 list of the most influential people of the 20th Century. Now, it's time for a little reality check: Bart Simpson is an animated character of a yellow-skinned, 10-year-old nihilist with spiky hair and a slick set of catchphrases. He's not Mother Theresa of Calcutta, Oscar Schindler, or Neil Armstrong. Yet, so many people have identified with this two-dimensional serial hell-raiser that he has evolved into an internationally recognised symbol of rebellion, even finding a profile in various real-life political campaigns around the world. Few in Malta will forget the bumper-sticker in 2005 of Bart Simpson baring his buttocks in opposition to the country joining the EU.

You really couldn't make it up.

He may be only 10 years old, but Bart Simpson could out-Menace Dennis and still not stop to draw breath. He's a kid with a sozzled, though well-meaning, dunderhead for a dad and a mother who, while recognising his negative qualities, can't think of Bart as anything other than her misunderstood "Special Little Guy".

Beneath the rebel, though, is Bart the Kind-Hearted. He often shows a genuine remorse for his misdoings but tends to get caught up in the moment. Several glimpses into the future over the years invariably see Bart as a 20-something lovable bum, the eternal moocher.

Without a doubt, Bart's hero-worship of the less-than-moral Krusty the Clown has added to his growing pains but it is an unredeemable cynic indeed who regards Bart Simpson as anything other than a 'loveable rogue'.

Killer trivia: In the TV show, Bart's everyday T-shirt is orange. However, on merchandise the shirt is normally blue to thwart counterfeiters. A tongue-in-cheek reference was once made to this in the Season 12 episode *Pokey Mom*.

Lisa Marie Bartzina Simpson

Lisa Simpson is 8, going on 43, certainly not your average second-grader. A brilliant student, a gifted sax player,  and one of life's philosophers, Lisa's spiky head is practically bursting with grandiose ideas and a sophistication that seem at odds with the rest of the Simpson clan. Let's not kid ourselves, Lisa knows she's smarter than anyone else on their street. This occasionally makes her a little high-minded and arrogant, but she also has a rebellious streak that she shares with Bart.

Away from home, Lisa is often famed for her Left Wing moral crusades that have resulted in, among other things, becoming an animal rights activist and supporter of the Free Tibet Movement.

Lisa is a Buddhist and a strict vegetarian, her mentor being an African-American saxophonist by the name of **'Bleeding Gums' Murphy**. Her size belies the singing voice of a 60-a-day *chanteuse* and she plays more instruments than she has fingers (which admittedly makes that claim to fame less impressive than it might be).

If it were possible for an animated character in a lampshade dress and string of pearls to become Leader of the Free World, then suggest the smart money would be on this power-packed bundle of brains.

Killer trivia: Lisa has an imaginary Jewish friend called Rachel Cohen. Ironically even her imaginary friends are nerds.

Margaret 'Maggie' Simpson, a.k.a. The Other Kid

It's a common misconception that baby Maggie Simpson doesn't talk. In fact, she talks a lot, as exemplified in the Season 3 episode *Brother, Can You Spare Two Dimes?*

where Homer's brother, Herb (voiced by Danny DeVito), invents a baby-talk translator. The problem is that, before this, everyone thought that Maggie did nothing all day but suck on her dummy and watch the rest of the family with a bemused expression on her face. Without the aid of technology, Maggie once said "Da-Da" under her own steam, but there was nobody around to hear her. In the episode *Lisa's First Word* Maggie was heard to be talking with the voice of movie diva Elizabeth Taylor.

One of Maggie's most notorious exploits was when she saved the life of thousands of plants, and the jobs of many weather reporters, by accidentally shooting billionaire Montgomery Burns thereby foiling his evil scheme to block the sun. Little Maggie is a demon of the Springfield BowlORama and an expert swimmer but, inexplicably, has been a baby of indeterminate age since 1987.

Killer trivia: In the skewed world of *The Simpsons*, even Maggie has an arch enemy, a mono-browed toddler called Gerald.

Family Ties

Of course, even The Simpsons have an extended family. Just as a bluffer would expect, they are a diverse and dysfunctional lot. Odd appearances have been made by Homer's mum, Mona (on the run from the FBI), his brother, Herbert (millionaire businessman from Detroit), and long-lost English sister, Abbie, but the core Simpson clan resides within Springfield's city limits.

Abraham J. Simpson – As far as most people are concerned, Abe Simpson – Homer's father – is just a senile old man who lives at the Springfield Retirement

Castle (motto: 'We thank you for not discussing the out-side world') with the other shrivelled geezers. However, Abe's life is more Bohemian than this and he's not merely a coffin-dodger with a head like an old coconut.

 Since his marriage collapsed after his wife, Mona Simpson, fled from the FBI in the 1960s, Abe has in turn lived on his own farm, at Homer's house, and finally in the retirement castle. With little else to occupy his twilight years, Abe enjoys boring the pants of anyone who will listen. He's like Mogadon in carpet slippers.

Many of Abe's anecdotes are fanciful and often more fiction than fact. However, his rambling senility belies a glorious military career as one of the Flying Hellfish. Sidelined – often cruelly – by his family, Abe now whiles away his days bitching, whining, and waiting for the tapioca pudding to turn up.

Killer trivia: Abe is President of the Gay and Lesbian Alliance according to a card he finds in his wallet, although he has no idea how that came to be.

Patricia Bouvier and Selma Bouvier-Terwilliger-Hutz-McClure-Stu-Simpson a.k.a. Patty and Selma

Marge Simpson's two older sisters, Patty and Selma are a pair of chain-smoking twin harridans obsessed with the old American adventure series *MacGyver*. The show's star, actor Richard Dean Anderson, was once kidnapped by the gruesome twosome and held captive in their apartment.

They both work at the Department of Motor Vehicles (DMV) and have a strong dislike of Homer. It is Selma who has married, in turn, **Sideshow Bob**, **Lionel Hutz**, **Troy McClure**, **Disco Stu** (a jive-talkin', bushy-haired, medallion-wearing disco addict) and **Abe Simpson**.

Patty remains discontentedly on the shelf and in fact came out as a lesbian in the Season 16 episode *There's Something About Marrying*.

Killer trivia: Selma is eldest by two minutes. The two can be identified by the fact that Selma has round, purple earrings while Patty's are orange and triangular.

Friends and neighbours

With buddies like these, who needs enemies? Most of Homer Simpson's pals are barflies from Moe's Tavern but they are good to have around when the Duff runs dry. By design or coincidence, Homer's drunken cronies all work with him at the Springfield Nuclear Power Plant.

Barney Gumble – Former and then born-again alcoholic, Barney has been Homer's best friend since childhood. Barney could generally be found propping up the bar – or vice-versa – at Moe's Tavern until the 11th Season episode *Days of Wine and D'oh-ses* when Barney is given a gift certificate for helicopter flying lessons. The old Barney was renowned for his drunken belch; the most interesting thing about the new one was his carefully coiffed hair. However, by Season 18, Barney was back on the bottle.

Before his introduction to Duff in high school, Barney was an articulate, well managed young man with a future and a tenor singing voice that could make the angels weep. The formidable fermentation has a lot to answer for.

Carl Carlson – Along with Julius Hibbert, Homer's work buddy and former supervisor, Carl is one of the few African-American characters in *The Simpsons*. Rarely seen without his best friend **Lenny** (Leonard), Carl would appear to be the more intelligent of the two, although Lenny has a Masters Degree.

Lenny Leonard – Lenny is Homer's co-worker at the Springfield Nuclear Power Plant and also one of his bar buddies. Lenny once kept a roof over his head by living in empty houses that were up for sale.

Moe Szyslak – Even though he has a face like a boxer dog chewing a wasp, Moe is one of Springfield's most beloved citizens. Well, beloved by the losers who inhabit his bar every night anyway. Unlucky in love (Moe has had an unrequited crush on Marge Simpson since high school), unlucky in life. With questionable personal hygiene, it's no wonder that Moe's demeanour means that he's 40-something, terminally single, and would be on suicide watch by the bar-flies if they could focus on him through the Duff-induced haze.

In one memorable episode, Moe had plastic surgery, which opened the door for him to become a soap star. Unfortunately, the door fell on him before the final credits, returning him to his original misshapen visage.

Nedward 'Ned' Flanders – The Simpson's next door neighbour, Ned is a good Christian man. Some say he's so virtuous that even God wouldn't want him. God – who has

put in one or two appearances in the show over the years – agrees. Ned is certainly a testament to religion-spurred health. At the tender age of 60, he looks no older than 40, despite his 'soup strainer' (moustache).

Ned is known for his obsessively religious fervour, going to church daily, raising his two sons as hard-working and devoted Christians, and helping anyone in need of comfort. He also has a really annoying pattern of speech.

Of Springfield's two left-handed-only stores, he owns the Leftorium, the best one this side of Leftopolis, where anybody with a sob story goes – not actually to buy anything, but because this Soft Touch will happily hand out free parking.

Maude Flanders – Ned's long-suffering wife and mother to Todd and Rod. Well, long-suffering, that is, until she died in a nasty T-shirt accident at a football game in the Season 11 episode *Alone Again Natura-diddly*. The salient point here is that Maude Flanders has the curious honour to be the only regular animated character in the history of television to have been killed off because the actress who voiced her left the show. A useful addition to your arsenal.

Todd and **Rod Flanders** – The eerie sons of Ned. Their ages, 8 and 10, seem to be interchangeable depending on which episode they appear in. Bart delights in shocking the devout siblings at every opportunity.

Apu Nahasapeemapetilon – The Asian corner shop owner. If Apu doesn't have it, then you probably don't need it. Just be prepared to pay over the odds for it and not to worry unduly about the Best Before date.

Perhaps no other shopkeeper has survived at least eight gun-shot wounds, has the mental prowess to work 18-hour-plus work-shifts, or has been the top student in a graduating class of one million. Apu was also the only known Hindu in Springfield until he married his wife Manjula and had 8 beautiful babies. Joking and amiable, Apu has many friends, from Homer to fellow Indian Sanjay. He is also a founding member of the Be-Sharps barbershop quartet.

The happiest days of his life

Bart Simpson is fortunate in that he is leader of his own particular pack at Springfield Elementary School. The fourth grade hell-raiser prefers to keep his friends close and his enemies even closer.

Milhouse Mussolini Van Houten – Bart's best friend and Lisa's wannabe beau. Son of Kirk (twice married to snooty Louann), Millhouse's emerging alternative sexuali-

ty is hinted at throughout the show, so when he finds himself a girlfriend (albeit short-term) it's a surprise to everyone – including a somewhat miffed Bart.

Milhouse is the nerdy asthmatic with the thick glasses who usually ends up getting beaten up at school. It's not much help to him that he has blue hair.

Dolphin 'Dolph' Starbeam, Coleby Corky James 'Jimbo' Jones, and **Kearney Zzyzwicz** – school bullies.

Martin Prince Jr – Son of stockbroker Martin Prince Sr, he's a super-intelligent, mega-enthusiastic schoolmate.

Nelson Muntz – Although another one of the predators in Bart's school-life, bully Nelson has a poignant side to

him. He lives with his mother, a former topless waitress, in a shack. His father left for a packet of cigarettes many years ago and never came back until the Muntz family were reunited by the Simpsons.

His Alpha Male bad attitude in the playground is backed up by a gang consisting of Jimbo, Kearney (who is in his 20s but still hangs about the school) and Dolph. He also once had a sister but he thinks she's probably dead.

Principle Seymour Skinner – Nobody could blame the principal of Springfield Elementary School for being a little odd. First of all he lives with his elderly mother, à la Norman Bates in Hitchcock's *Psycho*, and secondly he's been living a lie for decades. The real Seymour Skinner was believed to have died in Vietnam and was replaced by a well-meaning lookalike subordinate called Armin Tamzarian – his mother, Agnes, was too senile to spot the difference. The deception only came to light when the real Skinner returned to Springfield years later. The residents showed the depth of respect they had for the man they called their principal by choosing him over the real one and he stayed on as "Skinner".

As seems to be the case with many of Springfield's educators, Seymour is jaded and cynical but maintains a brave face and a devotion to duty. Once romantically linked to Patty Bouvier but dumped, he is now engaged to:

Edna Krabappel (pronounced 'krah-bar-pill') – Despite Bart Simpson and his teacher being constantly at logger-heads, there is a touching connection between Edna and her pupil. She once had a steamy romance by letter with Bart, who was impersonating a middle-aged man from a lonely hearts column, but in the Season 8 episode *Grade School Confidential* became romantically involved with Skinner. She is one of those teacher's that acts as if she lost all will to teach long ago. Edna was once caught in a compromising position with Skinner in a supplies cup-board. She's made it clear she's desperate for a man, which her class uses to full advantage.

Lunch Lady Doris – Works at Springfield Elementary School and is the mother of Squeaky Voiced Teen Jeremy

Peterson, although this has only ever been implied. This snippet, confidently produced, would impress the bluffee to the point of oxygen deprivation.

Otto Mann – If ever there was a less politically correct character in *The Simpsons*, it would be Otto the elementary school bus driver. Heavy metal fan Otto is a serial substance abuser and was once engaged to a woman called Becky who tried to murder Marge.

Groundskeeper Willie (whose brother is called Gravedigger Billy) is Springfield Elementary School's favourite janitor (well, only janitor to be honest), a grunting, red-haired caricature of a Scotsman, but all the better

 for it. At various times he has harboured a psychotic hatred of Bart (*Girly Edition*) and been given a successful Eliza Doolittle makeover by Lisa (*My Fair Laddy*). Despite being a fictional character, Grounds-keeper Willie came 8th in *The Glasgow Herald*'s 2003 poll of The Most Scottish Person in the World.

And the best of the rest (assorted weirdos)

Of course, any bluffers worth their salt could remember details about the main characters, but being a Simpsons' bluffer isn't that convenient.

Unlike any other animated TV family, the Simpsons' world is populated by hundreds of other characters, who range from "mildly eccentric" to "downright bonkers" on the Weirdo Scale. This list is by no means comprehensive but will offer the bluffer a working insight into just how complex the Simpsons' lives are. It would seem that the creative talent behind *The Simpsons* are playing mind games with the show's audience. Since the beginning there has been a whole army of supporting characters, many of whom make almost subliminal appearances in most episodes. The skill is to spot them.

In order to avoid any hard work, you need a quick run down. NB: several of the show's characters are never referred to by their given names during the usual course of events – Comic Book Guy and Sea Captain to name but two – but they do have first and family names (**Jeff Albertson** and **Capt Horatio McCallister** respectively). Stun your audience into submission by casually informing them that Crazy Cat Lady (the one whose role is simply to be a stereotypical elderly crazy person who screams incoherent abuse and throws her cats at other characters) was born Eleanor Abernathy.

Warning: The following list of *Simpsons* celebrities and their associated trivia is best left to Advanced Bluffers or those whose fear of being exposed as a rank amateur leads them to a reckless disregard for their own mental state.

Comic Book Guy – He's fat, he's 40, he's never had a girlfriend. He does have a ponytail and a store full of goodies called The Android's Dungeon.

This cuddly big kid has an encyclopedic knowledge of comics and the sci-fi-oriented merchandise in his store. His bad attitude to his (usually juvenile) customers is illustrated through his deep sarcasm and disdain for any-one who doesn't know their R2D2 from their Jah-Jah Binks*. He may not be one of Springfield's movers and shakers, and perhaps his misogyny can be irritating, but at least you can now advise others, with a degree of confi-dence, where to go to in a crisis for a copy of *Radioactive Man* #1.

* Annoying CGI character from the *Star Wars* movies.

Kenny Brockelstein a.k.a. **Kent Brockman** – Vain, silver-haired, anchorman on KBBL-TV.

BumbleBee Man a.k.a. **Pedro Chesperito** – Odd apparently Hispanic KMEX TV star who dresses in a huge bumble-bee suit which he never takes off, even when home alone. Speaks only in Spanish but is revealed to be actually British. Eccentricity being the Brits' stock in trade, what else could one expect?

Fat Tony a.k.a. **Marion Anthony D'Amico** (alias William Williams, Anthony Balducci) – Springfield's notorious mafia crime boss. With more than a nod to *The Godfather*, 'Fat Tony' spreads fear and havoc throughout the town. His rackets include ridding Springfield of salty snacks, bootlegging beer during Springfield's short-lived prohibition and supplying the schools with rat's milk.

Duffman – Actor, dressed as fake super-hero, who promotes Duff Beer with quite uncalled-for passion.

Prof John Frink – If geeks had a god, then Professor Frink would be the Archangel. Invariably dressed in a lab coat, Prof Frink has invented everything from a time machine to Lisa's self-tapping tap shoes.

Lionel Hutz – Shady lawyer who runs the "I Can't Believe It's A Law Firm!" legal practice. He disappeared from the show after the Season 10 episode *Bart the Mother* following the real-life murder of Phil Hartman, the actor who played him.

Gil Gunderson – We've all met a Gil in our lifetime. He's the terminally bad salesman who is always just one step away from that killer close. Unfortunately the step is the size of Antarctica.

Dr Julius Hibbert – Dr Hibbert is responsible for Bart Simpson. Not in the paternal sense, of course, but rather as the medical practitioner who delivered the screaming bundle of dynamite. Dr Hibbert is a major figure in the Springfield community and one of the few African-American residents. The well respected doctor is best known for chuckling mindlessly at the most inappropriate times. As a part of the upper class of Springfield, Dr Hibbert enjoys a balanced life, a job he cares for, and a one of a kind personality.

Clancy Wiggum – Springfield's porcine-faced Chief of Police. Wiggum's rotund figure makes him fairly useless at catching crooks but very good at the "eating-the-donuts" part of policing. In fact, the places on Springfield that have the lowest incidences of crime are the fast food outlets. Assisted by his two marginally more intelligent officers, Lou and Eddie, it's a scary thought that Wiggum controls law and order in the town. Even the most basic police jargon mystifies this crusader for justice; for example, who would trust a police chief who confuses 'DWI' (Driving Whilst Intoxicated) with 'DOA' (Dead on Arrival)?

Ralph Wiggum – Son of Police Chief Wiggum and a sweet-natured second-grader blessed with a huge imagination but without the intellectual wherewithal to channel it. That *The Simpsons* flies in the face of convention by featuring the educationally sub-normal Ralph, is a ground-breaking bonus to the show. Ralph would have a crush on classmate Lisa but doesn't know what a crush is. Speculate that either he's an embryonic psychopath or that he will end up succeeding his dim father as Springfield's Chief of Police. Or both.

Itchy & Scratchy – Ultra-violent cartoon characters featured on *The Itchy & Scratch Show*, based very loosely on *Tom & Jerry* and beloved by Bart and Lisa. There was once an Itchy & Scratchy movie starring the dimwitted cat and psychotic mouse but because of his bad behaviour, Bart doesn't get to see it until a 'flash-forward' segment when he is a middle-aged man.

Snake Jailbird – Springfield's main felon. If it's illegal then Snake has probably done it, from armed robbery to attempted (and successful) murder. He claims to be a former archaeologist and speaks in what the Americans call a "Valley Boy" accent.

Kang & Kodos – Large, green, tentacled aliens. They only usually appear in *The Simpsons'* annual *Treehouse of Horror* episodes. Named after characters in the original series of *Star Trek*.

Herschel Schmoikel Pinkus Krustofski a.k.a. **Krusty The Clown** – Children's TV personality Krusty has gone from being a street mime artist in Tupelo, Mississippi, to being a media star on Channel 6, and finally a broken, chain-smoking, jaded alcoholic who lives only for the spotlight, his vast collection of pornography, and to recoup

the millions he lost when the tax man finally caught up with him.

Apart from his three-hour-ten-minute kids' TV show (now cancelled), Krusty's empire has included a chain of KrustyBurger fast food restaurants, questionable and dangerous merchandise, premium rate phone lines, and a kids camp that was so bad he had to take all the campers on a free trip to Tijuana to make amends.

Sideshow Bob (Robert Underdunk Terwilliger) – He's a psychopath and he's a clown, so there's not much to like about Sideshow Bob. The highly intelligent predecessor of **Sideshow Mel**, Bob has spent every day since trying to frame his ex-boss Krusty the Clown for armed robbery, planning his revenge on the reason for his murderous flop, Bart Simpson, and just about anyone or anything else he feels is responsible for his many failures, including his Bad Hair Days.

Voiced by *Frazier* actor Kelsey Grammer, he is occasionally joined by *Frazier* co-star David Hyde-White, who voices Sideshow Bob's brother, Cecil.

Sea Captain – Ancient mariner who usually shows up whenever the show takes a nautical turn.

Troy McClure – Troy McClure is a splendid homage to all those small-time actors who make a couple of really bad films and then spend the rest of their careers churning out public information films while "having projects in development".

Hans Moleman – An elderly, bespectacled man who keeps dying in a phenomenon that has become known as The Many Deaths of Hans Moleman, but who is resurrected in time for the next episode.

Dr Marvin Munroe – Springfield's resident psychiatrist. Believed to be deceased by Season 6, he appears 10 years later explaining that he had just been seriously ill.

'Bleeding Gums' Murphy – African-American saxophonist and mentor of Lisa Simpson who is revealed to be the half-brother of **Dr Julius Hibbert**. Dies in the Season 6 episode *Round Springfield* and only Lisa attends his funeral.

Rev Timothy Lovejoy – As head of The First Church of Springfield, Reverend Lovejoy's sermons could bore the hind legs off a donkey, or any other Biblical creature. At  heart, even though the Simpsons favourite clergyman seems to exude a 'production line' philosophy to his Bible-bashing, deep down the committed Christian remains. Timothy Lovejoy is married to **Helen**, the town gossip, and has a bratty daughter, Jessica, who was voiced by Meryl Streep.

Squeaky Voiced Teen a.k.a. **Jeremy Peterson** – The offspring of **Lunch Lady Doris**. There are many Simpsons' 'squeaky voiced teens'. It's a character that has become a template for anyone in a McJob (but is one who has evolved enough to get his own name and a recurring role).

Radioactive Man & **Fallout Boy** – Springfield's answer to Batman & Robin.

Dr Nick Riviera – Backstreet quack who specialises in everything from dentistry to dog neutering.

Agnes Skinner – Principal Skinner's (Armin's) elderly mother. She's a vicious old crone who enjoys nothing more than treating her 45-year-old son as though he were 10. While usually portrayed berating him for something or other, Agnes occasionally pops up in odd stand-alone scenes as, for example, a member of a baying mob, or in little mini-adventures of her own.

Artie Ziff – Nerdy ex-date of Marge's who became a software billionaire. Doesn't resemble Microsoft's Bill Gates one little bit, no sir!

C. **Montgomery Burns** – The 104-year-old CEO of the Springfield Nuclear Power Plant is a wizened old geezer with more power – and money – than sense. His estranged mother, Daphne Charles Burns, is 122 years old. He has swindled and stomped his way to the top, ably abetted by a series of lickspittles, not least of which is Waylon J. Smithers Jr, whom he treats like the son he never wanted.

At the click of one of his bony fingers, Monty Burns can fire thousands of employees, and buy anything he wants...except love. He never seems to remember it but of all his thousands of employees, Homer Simpson seems to be the one whose life seems to be inextricably linked with his. Burns was once accidentally shot by Homer's baby daughter, Maggie.

Waylon J. **Smithers Jr** – Smithers is a rarity in animation. Well, maybe not that rare. Maybe a "one in ten". Monty Burns' sidekick lives alone, collects Malibu Stacey dolls (the Springfield version of Barbies), and enjoys nothing more than taking part in a Gay Pride march. Like the Clark Kent/Superman thing, nobody in the series has so far made the only logical connection. NB: He was a black character for his first appearance in the show. Nobody has ever explained why.

Homer once stood in for Waylon Smithers when he took his first ever vacation. Smithers has something of an unrequited longing for his wrinkly boss, which is primarily disguised by his devotion to his job.

Sideshow Mel a.k.a. **Melvin Van Horne** – It's not easy to miss the eloquent and erudite Mel. He usually wears only a furry loin-cloth (no, really!) though occasionally a suit, but he always, always has a large bone through his emerald-hued bee-hive. Mel is the reluctant stooge to

Krusty the Clown and his primary role is to show indignation at the exploits of various Springfield residents.

Mayor Joseph 'Diamond Joe' Quimby – He's a sleazy, womanising, crook. Not at all like any American presidents of recent history. Oh no.

Diverting public funds to his own coffers, the murder of his enemies, being unfaithful to his wife, drug addictions, and supporting an unfair law against illegal immigrants are just some of Diamond Joe's less-than-illustrious activities. Inexplicably he's kept his job for over a decade, so there must be something about this Kennedy-esque buffoon that the folk of Springfield relate to.

Rainier Luftwaffe Wolfcastle – Whether Arnold Schwarzenegger gets the joke of Rainier Wolfcastle or not, nobody knows, but Bart's hero is basically an animated version of the musclebound actor and politician. Wolfcastle has a daughter called Greta and a many-times married wife called Maria-Schriver-Kennedy-Quimby.

Cletus Del Roy Spuckler – Cletus the Slack-Jawed Yokel is the simple, well-meaning husband of Brandine and father of … wait for it… Birthday, Brandine, Brittany, Caitlin, Cassidy, Chloe, Crystal Meth, Cody, Cubert, Dermot, Dylan, Heather, Hunter, Gummy Sue, Ian, Incest, International Harvester, Lauren, Jitney, Jordan, Kendall, Kyra, Max, Morgan, Noah, Phil, Rubella Scabies, Rumer, Sacha, Scout, Taylor, Tiffany, W, Wesley, Witney, and Zoe. If that wasn't enough, the family circle at one time included an old hound-dog called Geetch.

Brandine Spuckler – Trailer trash wife of Cletus. At last count Brandine had 36 children with probably more on the way.

BE OUR GUEST – THE GREAT AND THE GOOD CALL ON THE SIMPSONS

You know when you have a runaway success on your hands when your cast looks like the guest list to the Oscars, Emmys and Baftas rolled into one. The following is by no means comprehensive, but illustrates the esteem in which *The Simpsons* is held around the world. And this list only includes internationally-known names – if those known primarily in the US were included, the roll-call would treble.

You might even want to turn this into something of a game. Imagine the Smartie-point potential of creating *Simpsons*-themed charades where someone has to act out the name of the guest star. Take your pick from:

Andre Agassi, Anne Bancroft, Alec Baldwin, Barry White, Bette Midler, Blink-182, Bob Newhart, Britney Spears, Brook Shields, Buzz Aldrin (the astronaut), Tom Jones, Danny DeVito, David Duchovney, Dolly Parton, Donald Sutherland...

William Shatner, Patrick McGoohan, Drew Barrymore, Dustin Hoffman, Elton John, Dr Phil (self-help guru from the *Oprah Winfrey Show*), Elliot Gould, Glenn Close, Gore Vidal, Hugh Hefner, James Caan, Johnny Cash, Mark Hamill, Jerry Lewis, Lisa Kudrow, Martin Sheen, Matthew Perry, The Who, Meg Ryan, Elizabeth Taylor (both as voice talent and herself) ...

Michelle Pfeiffer, Ernest Borgnine, James Brown, Mick Jagger, Paul Newman, Eric Idle, Red Hot Chili Peppers, Richard Gere, Paul McCartney, Stephen King (author), Sting, Pierce Brosnan, Rupert Murdoch, Pete Samprass, Peter Bogdanovich, Ricky Gervais, Natalie Portman, Simon Cowell, Steven Hawking (twice), Ted Danson, Susan Sarandon, Ian McKellan, J. K. Rowling, Jack Lemmon, U2...

BART AND MOE CRANK IT UP...

One of the many highlights from *The Simpsons* seasons are Bart's crank phone calls to his nemesis, Springfield's manic depressive bartender, Moe Szyslak. The risqué nature of some of these calls notwithstanding, some may ask why a 10-year-old boy indulges in such tomfoolery. This is where your bluffing skills will be truly put to the test. The rationale behind Bart's actions has never been fully explained other than Bart is a pest and Moe is... well, stupid and falls for it every time. Don't suggest looking for Orwellian metaphor here – this is *The Simpsons* and sometimes the laughs are simply what they are.

The format of these little vignettes is deceptively clever. Bart calls Moe's bar and asks to speak to a fictitious customer. Moe calls out the name of the customer to the assembled – usually drunk – company and only then realises what he's been conned into saying.

It is claimed that this running gag originated in the Tube Bar, Jersey City, in the 1970s but it's obvious even to the most intellectually challenged of neighbouring Shelbyville that these gems go further back than that and are based in classic 'knock-knock' jokes – 'Knock-knock/who's there?/ Isobel/Isobel who?/Isabel necessary on a bicycle?' With a grandiose wave of your four yellow digits, explain this sagely to your bluffee and then bask in glory as their respect-ometer rises exponentially.

Bart's made-up names are usually juvenile and predictable but never cease to be funny to those whose sense of humour will forever remain in the snot-encrusted limbo of primary school. If you fancy your chances of walking in the footsteps of Grand Master Bart, a prerequisite is a victim who has an IQ of a peanut. An estate agent or topless model might be a good start, but we'd think twice about taking on championship boxers, if we were you.

To inspire in your quest for eternal Bart-dom, try:

Moe: Uh, is I.P. Freely here? Hey, everybody, I.P. Freely!

Moe: Hey, is there a Butz here? Seymour Butz? Hey, everybody, I wanna Seymour Butz!

Moe: B. O'Problem. B. O'Problem. Hey, do I have a B. O'Problem here?
Barney: You sure do!

Moe: Uh, Homer Sexual? Aw, come on, come on, one of you guys has gotta be Homer Sexual!
Homer: Don't look at me!

Moe: Uh, Hugh Jass? Oh, somebody check the men's room for a Hugh Jass!

Moe: Uh, Amanda Huggenkiss? Hey, I'm looking for Amanda Huggenkiss! Ah, why can't I find Amanda Huggenkiss?
Barney: Maybe your standards are too high!

Moe: Mike Rotch! Mike Rotch! Hey, has anybody seen Mike Rotch lately?

Moe: Telegram for Heywood U. Cuddleme! Heywood U. Cuddleme? Big guy in the back, Heywood U. Cuddleme?

Once you've tracked your victim with the stealth of a genetically enhanced leopard, the results are usually well worth the effort and will provide hours of fun if you work for MI5 and have access to phone bugging technology.

A note of caution, though. "Who knows Ivor Biggun?" will have been done the world over and won't impress anybody.

31

LOST HORIZON – SO WHERE EXACTLY IS SPRINGFIELD?

The truth is that nobody really knows. No – they really don't. The more philosophical of its adherents will claim that the place the Simpsons call home is located at the furthest reaches of the Dark Place known as creator Matt Groening's psyche. However, that's patently nonsense. The bluffer can proclaim with chest puffed out and head high, nowhere can be that remote.

The skilled bluffer might even be able to engage in a little cerebral judo with *Simpsons* enthusiasts by using the fact that nobody really knows against them. Why not turn it into a game, the solution to which, your face will imply, is known only to you?

Over the years, several hints have been dropped about Springfield:

- It is somewhere on the North American continent (well a version of it anyway);
- It has a coastline from which the traveller may reach international waters;
- It has mountain ranges, prairies, forested areas, meadows, canyons, swamps, a desert and an active volcano;
- It has an Army base, a Naval base, an Airforce base and two old forts – For Springfield and Fort Sensible;
- The nearest town is called Shelbyville but only really stupid people live there;
- The State capital is called Capital City (nicknamed The Windy Apple);

Major geographic features include Mount Springfield, Mount Embolism, the Murderhorn, Springfield National Forest, the Springfield Badlands (a.k.a the Alkali Flats), Springfield Gorge, and Springfield Glacier. Catfish Lake is known for its fishing and marriage retreats; Geezer Rock was unwittingly destroyed by Homer Simpson.

Rattle these facts off in quick succession to unsuspecting devotees and then challenge them to point to Springfield on a map. You can make the prize as extravagant as you want, of course, because they will fail miserably. It's geographically impossible for any town to meet these criteria. They stand more chance of sticking their pin in the Land of Oz.

All one can say for certain is that whichever state Springfield is in, it's bordered by Ohio, Nevada, Maine, and Kentucky, as explained by Ned Flanders in *The Simpson's Movie*. Relate this nugget to new fans and watch the part of their brain that deals with geography grind into action trying to locate the illusive state. While Kentucky and Ohio border each other, Maine is 1500 miles north east, and Nevada 2000 miles west.

For a little extra ammunition, you can mention the groundbreaking segment *Homer³*, where the devious animators actually created a three-dimensional Homer Simpson and dumped him onto a real street via a wormhole. The newly inflated and invigorated Homer then proceeds to interact with the bemused citizens of Real America. Who was the more horrified by this collision of cultures remains a matter for future historians but might provide a kudos-engendering point of debate for bluffers.

Of course, the truth is that the Simpsons and the town where they live are fictional. The whole point is that we're not supposed to be able to solve the riddle. Springfield doesn't have a real state, and the fact that it has no state is just a running gag. Springfield is 'Anytown, USA'; a chimera of every town and every state in America. Springfield is nowhere and everywhere…

In the US, there are no fewer than 71 towns called 'Springfield', which is why Simpsons creator Matt

Groening used the name. Incidentally, it is not the most common by any means. For that, you can cite the 275 towns that share the name 'Fairview'.

For those who insist that Springfield's state is real but as yet undisclosed, simply tell them this: you will give them one million pounds if they can tell you the American state whose state capital is called Capital City. That should shut them up for a while.

However, in the fictional world of *The Simpsons*, the state has a Springfield County in which the town of Springfield is located. There is also a Swartzwelder County, which borders Springfield County, and the very rural Spittle County, for which the banjo music from the movie *Deliverance* might have been written.

Other cities in the state include: Cypress Creek, founded by the Globex Corporation; Ogdenville, famous for its outlet malls; and Little Pwagmattasquarmsettport, America's scrod basket. There are also towns with chilling names such as Terror Lake, Bloodbath Gulch, Ghost Town, Cape Fear, New Horrorfield, and Screamville, and towns with the chaste names of Frigid Falls, Mount Seldom and Lake Flaccid.

History of Springfield

Early Days

Popular lore has it that Springfield was founded in 1796 by circus freaks from Maryland who, misinterpreting a passage in the Bible, thought they were heading for a little home from home called New Sodom. Instead, the pilgrims founded Springfield, based on more Puritan ethics. Neighbouring Shelbyville, Springfield natives will attest, was based on how many of their own close relatives they could marry.

The town's founding father was Jebediah Obadiah

Zachariah Jedediah Springfield, a murderous pirate and enemy of George Washington, widely celebrated in the town as a patriotic American hero. He tamed a wild buffalo and killed a bear with his bare hands, and his deeds are immortalised with a bronze statue that stands proudly in front of the Springfield Town Hall.

The town's first motto 'A noble spirit embiggens the smallest man' is attributed to Jebediah, but has since been replaced by *Corruptus In Extremis* during the administration of Mayor 'Diamond Joe' Quimby.

The state is a northern state that was on the Union side during the American Civil War. The fact that the state flag has a Confederate flag on it makes it all the more embarrassing for the population.

Present day

In *Bart-Mangled Banner*, Bart Simpson accidentally moons the United States flag, and the Simpsons appear on a talk show to explain the matter. However, the show's host makes it appear that Springfield hates America. When the rest of America reciprocates this loathing, Mayor Joe Quimby changes the name of Springfield to 'Liberty-Ville'. An enormous patriotic craze ensues, wherein all items *are* priced at $17.76, even houses. (Q: Why this sum? A: It's the date of the American War of Independence.)

Because of an area code dispute, for a brief period Springfield divided itself into two cities. Homer Simpson, thoroughly upset that he has to memorise a new area code (939) while the rich side of town retains the familiar 636 code, incites the lower class citizens of Springfield to rebel and establish their side as a separate town to be called New Springfield. They erect a wall made of refuse dividing the two area codes and elect Homer as their new mayor.

Mayor Quimby maintains control of the rich side, which *comes to be* called Old Springfield. The two towns reunite when the rock band The Who, while in town for a concert, suggests speed dial to solve Springfield's problem and agree to play if the wall is torn down (*A Tale of Two Springfields*).

At one point, Homer is elected as Sanitation Commissioner (*Trash of the Titans*). When Homer spends the entire annual budget in only his first month of office, the town is forced to take in the garbage of other cities in order to make enough money to pay their own city's trash collectors. Eventually the mines that are storing the collected trash overflow and litter spreads, prompting the entire city, population and structures, to move quite literally five miles down the road to establish 'new' Springfield away from the massive dump that 'old' Springfield had become.

When Mayor Quimby briefly skips town due to some 'missing' lottery funds, the town's MENSA chapter (Lisa Simpson, Dr Julius Hibbert, Lindsey Naegle, Comic Book Guy, and Prof Frink) take over. They change all the clocks in town to metric time, eliminate the green lights from stoplights, and put the city on the list of Top-300 US cities. It comes in at 299th.

Economy

Springfield's state is mainly agricultural it appears, with large cities and small- to medium-sized towns such as Springfield. The farms mainly produce corn, livestock, dairy, fruit, cotton, and tobacco. Within the cities, the main industries are brewing by the Duff and Fudd beer corporations, coal mining, and environmentally unfriendly power generation. Lesser industries include casinos, box manufacturing, pillows, food, copper, iron, steel, industrial equipment, retail and dangerous chemicals. It's an economic profile that guarantees that most of the population works in low paid jobs.

However, the local economy is not without its entrepreneurs, such as C. Montgomery Burns, Howard K. Duff VIII, Aristotle Amadopoulos, Goose Gladwell, Arthur Fortune, Hank Scorpio, and Artie Ziff. Most of these high-profile citizens have questionable business ethics.

Springfield includes both areas of high wealth (Old Springfield), and slum areas (New Springfield). Because of this, the town's inhabitants have become noticeably polarised with constant feuds between the upper and lower classes. There is also the unpopular community of Stenchburg.

The state of the State

The state is heavily polluted due to a history of sloppy environmental controls, various corrupt local government, greedy business and Mafia influence. Toxic waste is an everyday hazard, especially near the Springfield Nuclear Power Plant, and Lake Springfield contains mutated three-eyed fish. Despite this, the state has a wide array of wildlife – bald eagles and bears, not Sideshow Bob.

Springfield's Main Street is in a pitiful state of disrepair owing to citizens driving along it while carrying excessively heavy loads and leaving snow chains on their tyres after the snow has melted. (Homer Simpson has been spotted driving along it with a massive grand piano strapped to the roof of his car as his chain-covered tires gouged the pavement.) Some of the potholes have become so wide that cars have actually fallen into them.

Gambling is legal in Springfield, as is gay marriage, trade in children, and fishing with dynamite. There are a number of unusual statutes in Springfield and its town charter, including the chief constable "shall receive one pig every month and two comely lasses of virtue true".

Education

The state follows a standard American education system, with elementary schools, junior high schools and high schools. However, thanks to a very low education budget, schools can only afford to buy books other schools have banned, they are forced to cancel all artistic and physical education, and must rent out classrooms as prison cells to make ends meet.

Among others is Miss Tillingham's School for Snooty Girls and Mama's Boys, and an all-girls Catholic school run by French-Canadian nuns (Saint Sebastian's School for Wicked Girls). There are also a number of colleges, including the unfortunately acronymed Springfield Heights Institute of Technology.

Religion

The largest church community is the Presbylutheran church headed by the Reverend Lovejoy. Springfield also has Jehovah's Witnesses, a Jewish synagogue, an African American community church, a Catholic church, a Buddhist Temple and an Episcopal church (with vibrating pews). The Nahasapeemapetilons are Hindu and worship a statue of the god Ganesh in the backroom of Apu's Kwik-E-Mart store. Bart's school has a group of Amish students and, at one point, many Springfielders joined a cult group called the 'Movementarians' but, when it was revealed as a fraud, quickly moved on.

There is also the 'Stonecutters Lodge' (currently renamed 'The Ancient Society of No-Homers') of which practically every male in the city is a member – minus Homer Simpson.

BUSINESS IS BUSINESS –
THE BUCK STOPS HERE

Visitors to Springfield will be spoilt for choice when it comes to spending the almighty dollar. Among those establishments that attempt to cater to every need are:

- Androids' Dungeon (Comic book store)
- Blood Bath and Beyond (Gun Shop)
- Eastside Ruff-Form School; Professor Von Bowser's Sanatorium For Dogs (dog obedience schools)
- Eye Carumba (optician)
- French Confection (pastry shop)
- Helter Shelter (Soup kitchen)
- I Can't Believe It's A Law Firm! (legal practice)
- Karmaceuticals (New Age shop)
- King Toots (music shop)
- Lard Lad Donuts (doughnut shop)
- Malaria Zone (outdoor clothing store)
- Nuts Landing (dog neutering parlour)
- Repo Depot (repossession company)
- Saks Fifth Grade (girls' clothing store)
- Suicide Notes and Tommy Toots (music shop)
- The Lucky Stiff Funeral Home (undertaker)
- The Family Jewels (jewellery store)
- The Ritz Carlton Hotel for Vagrants (motel)
- Toys "L" Us (Chinatown toy store)
- Try 'n Save (discount store)
- Uriah's Heap (junkyard)
- Valley of the Dolls (toy store)
- Yuckingham Palace (joke/novelty shop)

Transport

Springfield's regular bus service has stops at Airport Refuelling Way, Area 51A and Cracktown. The bus depot is serviced by Buck-U-Bus, First Class Bus Lines and Sit 'n Stare. Charter bus service is available through Springfield Travel (slogan: 'Now get outta here!'), featuring trips to Dollywood.

The area has a good rail network and a subway system (never seen but mentioned in asides). Several international airports also provide a strong transport link with destinations in the state, other US states, and the world. Unfortunately for The World.

People and culture

It is widely believed that most of the inhabitants of Springfield are stupid, overweight, quick to anger, and heavily perverted. As described by Dr Julius Hibbert, it is a town where the smartest have no power and the stupidest run everything. *Time* magazine once did a cover story on Springfield entitled 'America's Worst City', and *Newsweek* has in the past referred to the city as 'America's Crud Bucket'. In addition, Springfield holds the record for World's Fattest Town and Most Heart Attacks. It is also meant to be the Meanest City of America.

The city has been the object of many lootings, as well, usually when there is a citywide blackout. The loopy folk of Springfield are easily inclined to riot, with some rioters going as far as to wield weapons. Mobs form very quickly and they usually march toward the object of their anger with pitchforks and flaming torches as their the weapons of choice, be it Springfield Town Hall, the local burlesque or, as is frequently the case, the Simpsons' house. Principal Seymour Skinner once proudly declared: "There's no justice like angry-mob justice."

Arts and entertainment

Springfield boasts an opera house, an outdoor amphitheatre, an arboretum, a vibrant jazz scene and was once mentioned as the entertainment capital of its state. The Concert Hall was closed down when everyone walked out after hearing the first few bars of Beethoven's Fifth finding classical music objectionable.

There is also an unusually high number of museums, including a Natural History museum, a stamp museum, Springfield Knowledgeum, The Museum of Swordfish, Springsonian Museum, and Springfield Museum (which features the world's largest cubic zirconia).

To the west of the city the main attraction is The World's Largest Toilet.

Sports

In addition to a dog track Springfield sport offers: the Springfield Isotopes AA baseball team (which once threatened to move to Albuquerque, New Mexico, where the real-life minor league baseball team eventually changed their name to the Isotopes), the Springfield Speedway, the Springfield Atoms football team (led by Stan 'The Boy' Taylor), the Springfield Stun arena football team, the Springfield Ice-otopes hockey team, the Association of Springfield Semi-Pro Boxers, and a Monster Truck Rally (featuring Truckasaurus).

There are also many intramural options available to children, including youth ice hockey, football, soccer and volleyball, but the most popular sport for children is baseball/softball. However when Marge once said at a town meeting, '...and I love baseball' the crowd booed. We can assume, however, that these outlets are greatly under funded, as one season of volleyball was cancelled after Lisa Simpson accidentally popped a ball with her pointed hair.

Crime

There are a number of prisons in Springfield, including Springwood Minimum Security Prison and Montgomery Burns State Penitentiary. Though never mentioned again after a school strike, Bart's school was turned into Springfield Elementary and Prison to help deal with money issues, but the final scene of the episode suggests that a prison break took place.

Several episodes, including *The Seven-Beer Snitch*, would seem to suggest that Springfield is located in a state that retains the death penalty, with both an electric chair and a gas chamber being depicted in some of the town's various correctional facilities. There is also a psychiatric care facility named 'Calmwood'.

The Springfield Police Department, led by Police Chief Clancy Wiggum, is a largely corrupt and incompetent organisation. Most of the time, it seems to have only three members (Wiggum, and beat cops Lou and Eddie).

On two occasions in the town's history, police duties have been removed from the Springfield Police Department:

1. On the first occasion, they were handed over to a posse of drunken vigilantes, led by Homer Simpson, in order to better protect the 'World's Largest Cubic Zirconia' from a cunning and charming cat burglar.

2. On the second occasion, they were transferred to the security company 'Springshield', again run by Homer, with the help of his friends Lenny and Carl.

Most of the organised crime in town is controlled by Sicilian mob boss Fat Tony and his bungling cronies. Fat Tony, however, makes a lot of gangster-type noises but nothing much ever comes of it. More din than Don, you might say.

TOP 20 SIMPSONS EPISODES

Wow them at parties by boldly reeling off beginnings, middles and ends to the best Simpsons shows, thereby implying to your admirers that you are quite capable, if pushed, of quoting every line from every show of each season chapter and verse. Just pray they don't push you.

Each Simpsons episode has its own production code – which is incomprehensible to anyone who doesn't have a degree in particle physics – and an honest-to-goodness title in (mostly) plain English. With over two decades of material to choose from, even the most skilled bluffer should resist attempting to memorise every episode title as the author is not responsible for any form of cerebral meltdown.

Without a doubt, some of the best Simpsons' episodes are those that feature songs (usually parodies of existing ones). Bluffers with an ambitious streak might want to hear the best at www.simpsonscrazy.com – and learn them. When you start singing these ditties word-perfect, your acolytes will either listen enraptured or rapidly move to where the booze is.

One Fish, Two Fish, Blowfish, Bluefish (Season 2)

Entreated by Lisa, the Simpsons decide to expand their dining horizons. After eating a poisonous blowfish at a Japanese restaurant, Homer discovers that he has only 24 hours to live. The final scene where Marge finds him apparently dead sitting in an armchair before a sunrise vista (kind of *Death in Venice* without the Mahler) is unexpectedly touching.

One Fish, Two Fish, Blowfish, Bluefish should convert even the most hardened *Simpsons* sceptic.

Memorable quote:
Lisa: Hmm...Friday night – pork chops. From cradle to

grave... etched in stone and God's library somewhere in Heaven.

Stark Raving Dad (Season 3)

Because of Bart, Homer is committed to a psychiatric hospital, where he meets a chubby white giant who claims to be singer Michael Jackson. On 'Michael's' release, he and Bart become friends and write a special Birthday song for Lisa.

Because of Michael Jackson poking fun at himself for a change, feel confident in proclaiming that *Stark Raving Dad* rates as one of – if not *the* – best episodes of *The Simpsons* ever produced. In a bizarre twist, Jackson provided the voice talent for the dialogue, but not the singing.

Song: Happy Birthday, Lisa!

Memorable quote:
MJ: [*over the 'phone to Bart*] I'm Michael Jackson.
Bart: *THE* Michael Jackson? No way!
MJ: It's true. I'm with your father in a mental institution.
Bart: Uh huh... And is Elvis with you?
MJ: Could be. It's a big hospital.

Colonel Homer (Season 3)

After a fight with Marge, Homer hides in an out-of-town redneck bar for solace. He meets a small-time country music star called Lurlene Lumpkin and becomes her manager. As the two are drawn closer closer and Lurlene is launched into stardom, Marge begins to suspect that Homer is being unfaithful to her.

Song: Your Wife Don't Understand You (But I Do)

Memorable quote:
Bart: Country music sucks. All it does is take precious air space away from shock DJs, whose cruelty and profanity amuse us all.

It's remarks like this that ensure the slavering devotion of the faithful.

Marge vs The Monorail (Season 4)

A travelling salesman in a straw hat manages to sell the good, if rather dim, folk of Springfield a substandard monorail. Everyone is delighted but Marge. Naturally nobody could have been chosen to be the driver but Homer, and chaos ensues when the controls jam. A guest appearance by *Star Trek*'s Leonard Nimoy as himself makes it all the more noteworthy.

Song: Monorail!

Memorable Quote:
Apu: I would like to see this money spent on more police officers. I have been shot eight times this year. As a result, I almost missed work.
Police Chief Wiggum: Cry-baby!

Krusty Gets Kancelled (Season 4)

Who would have thought that Bette Midler was one of Krusty the Clown's oldest and dearest showbiz chums? When the Clown Prince's show is cancelled in favour of a ventriloquist's dummy called Gabbo, it's Bette and the rest of Krusty's Kronies – sorry... cronies, including Barry White, Johnny Carson, Luke Perry, Hugh Hefner and The Red Hot Chili Peppers – who rush to his aid with a schmaltzy benefit concert.

Even *The Simpsons* is allowed to dampen a cheek or two when the occasion beckons.

Memorable quote:
Krusty: I don't know how to thank you kids.
Bart: That's all right, Krusty.
Lisa: We're getting fifty percent of the T-shirt sales.

Whacking Day (Season 4)
Not aired very often for some reason but well worth wait-ing for, *Whacking Day* is a surreal little piece where animal rights activist Lisa campaigns against the contin-uation of a charming little Springfield tradition that revolves around whacking snakes to death with any implement that comes to hand.

Song: Whacking Day Hymn

Memorable quote:
Miss Springfield: Gentlemen, start your whacking!

A Streetcar Named Marge (Season 4)
Marge gets herself a part in an amateur production based on *A Streetcar Named Desire* with next door neighbour Ned. In *Oh Streetcar!* Marge plays Blanche to Ned's bare-chested Stanley, but the play is so far Off Broadway that it's practically in Kentucky. It transpires that *Oh Streetcar!* has ominous parallels with the Simpsons' own life but Homer is too dim to see them.

Memorable quote:
Marge: I just don't see why Blanche should shove a broken bottle in Stanley's face. Couldn't she just take his abuse with gentle good humour?

Selma's Choice (Season 4)
Selma decides that she wants kids but the reality of taking Bart and Lisa to the Duff Gardens theme park changes her mind, especially when Lisa falls into the

contaminated beer river and proclaims herself "The Lizard Queen". The episode includes a quirky musical version of *Planet of The Apes*.

The theme park's animatronic figures singing *It's A Small World* are truly sinister and any attempt on behalf of the bluffer to imitate them should really be left until copious amounts of alcohol has been consumed for full effect.

Memorable quote:
Homer: Patty, Selma, I'm sorry. [*hugs them*]
Selma: He's hugging us. What do we do?
Patty: Just close your eyes and think of *MacGyver*.

Homer's Barbershop Quartet (Season 5)
Homer, Principal Skinner, Apu and Chief Wiggum reveal a surprise past – as chart-topping barbershop quartet, the Be-Sharps. The finale is a delicious nod to the Beatles' farewell appearance on the roof of the Apple building in London. George Harrison passes by in this scene saying: "It's been done." This is one of those rare *Simpsons* episodes that transcends the obvious humorous set-up and resolution and enters the world of *film noir*.

Song: Baby on Board

Memorable quote:
Lisa: Wow, an original Malibu Stacey from 1958! [*Sees the huge, pointed breasts*] Oh…
Man: Yeah, they took her off the market after some kid put both his eyes out. That'll teach boys to play with dolls…

22 Short Films About Springfield (7)
The episode is also rumoured to have sparked the idea among the staff of a spin-off TV series *Tales from*

Springfield, focusing on the town rather than the Simpsons, however the idea never took flight. The creative team felt it would detract from *The Simpsons* as a TV series, and that the show already focused sufficiently on the townsfolk. It is still debated whether or not this whole idea was just fan speculation.

Song: Cletus the Slack-Jawed Yokel

Memorable quote:
Rev Lovejoy: [*to his dog*] C'mon boy, this is the spot, right here. That's a good boy, do your dirty, sinful business.
Ned Flanders: Well, howdy, Reverend Lovejoy. Nice to see you there ... on my lawn ... with your dog.
Rev Lovejoy: Oh, oh, ooh, bad dog! Look at that, right on Ned's lawn. Now how could you do such a thing? [*quietly to the dog*] Good boy, don't stop now.

Simpsonscalifragilisticexpiali[annoyed grunt]cious   (8)
After Marge suffers from stress, The Simpsons get a nanny in the form of Shary Bobbins – no, absolutely no similarity between her and a certain Disney Corporation icon should be made or implied – who flies in and turns 742 Evergreen Terrace upside down with a wealth of twee magic and song. Naturally, the deliciously irreverent *It's The American Way*, in no way resembles *A Spoonful of Sugar* either. Litigation lawyers are not in awe of even Hollywood's creative giants.

Song: Minimum Wage Nanny

Memorable quote:
Shary: Hello, I'm Shary Bobbins.
Homer: Did you say Mary Po–
Shary: No, I definitely did not. I'm an original creation, like Rickey Rouse, or Monald Muck.

(EPISODE) NAMES TO DROP

A cursory glance at episode titles is almost as entertaining as the episodes themselves. More often than not, these little one-line gems parody something else in popular culture, be it literary, musical, televisual, or cinematic. Consider these as prime examples:

- Missionary: Impossible
- My Big Fat Geek Wedding
- Last Exit to Springfield
- The Last Temptation of Homer
- A Fish Called Selma
- Much Apu About Nothing
- You Only Move Twice
- The Canine Mutiny
- The Principal and the Pauper
- Trash of the Titans
- Lard of the Dance
- When You Dish Upon a Star
- Monty Can't Buy Me Love
- Guess Who's Coming to Criticize Dinner?
- Children of a Lesser Clod
- The Way We Weren't

This Little Wiggy (9)
Marge makes Bart befriend the oh-so-helpless young Wiggum. Bart is not too impressed until he finds that Ralph has access not only to his Police Chief dad's gun but also his pass key for all kinds of places, including the creepy Morningwood Penitentiary. When Bart turns on Ralph in favour of his tough friends, the scene is actually quite chilling and has echoes of *Lord of the Flies*.

Natural Born Kissers/Margie, May I Sleep With Danger (9)

Homer and Marge find they can spice up their love life by having sex in unusual places. One exploit finds them being discovered naked inside a crazy golf windmill and the middle of a crowded football field. Meanwhile, Bart and Lisa unearth the lost alternative ending to *Casablanca*. The title of this episode depends on whether shown on terrestrial or satellite television.

It's details like this that establish your credibility.

Memorable quote:

Lisa: Wow! An alternate ending to *Casablanca*. Bart, this could be priceless!

Bart: Priceless like a mother's love, or the good kind of priceless?

Simpsons Bible Stories (10)

It's a hot Sunday in the First Congregational Church of Springfield and Reverend Lovejoy is punishing his flock after finding a chocolate Easter Bunny in the collection plate. The Simpsons fall asleep and dream that they're Bible characters; Homer and Marge become Adam and Eve; Bart is David versus Goliath (Nelson); and Milhouse is Moses being pursued by the mighty armies of the Pharoah (Principal Skinner).

Memorable quote: Homer [*as Adam in the Garden of Eden*]: Oh, my dear, sweet Eve. I love you even more than the butterscotch pond or the porno bush.

Viva Ned Flanders (10)

Much to everyone's amazement, Homer's old adversary, Ned Flanders, reveals that he is 60 years old and regrets having done nothing with his life. Homer takes him to Las Vegas for the ultimate good time, where they both marry drunken casino prostitutes – their "Vegas Wives".

Memorable quote:
Ned: How do you do it, Homer? How do you silence that little voice that says "Think!"?
Homer: You mean Lisa?
Ned: Oh, no, I mean common sense.
Homer: Oh, that! That can be treated with our good friend alcohol! You might want to write that down...

Behind the Laughter (11)
The Simpsons step outside their usual roles and talk frankly about their turbulent life away from the TV cameras. It soon becomes clear that the reality is some-what different from rosy TV fantasy as old feuds and scandals rise to the surface.

Memorable quote: Lisa: [*interviewed in her room*] I had no business hosting the Oscars. After the show, Meryl Streep spat on me!

Faith Off (11)
Bart discovers evangelism. After removing a bucket of glue from Homer's head, he becomes a fake faith healer. However, his efforts to re-attach the leg of injured foot-ball star Anton Luchenko are less successful.

Saddlesore Galactica (11)
Bart becomes a jockey when he and Homer rescue a high-diving horse called Duncan from a circus. Re-named Furious D, the nag shows himself to be a world-class racehorse. Then the other jockeys (who are actually

evil elves in disguise, of course) try to intimidate owner Homer into throwing the race.

Memorable quote:

Chief Wiggum: I'd rather let a thousand guilty men go free than chase after them.

The Regina Monologues (15)

The Simpsons head to Great Britain where they're met at the airport by Tony Blair. Homer crashes his Mini into Her Majesty The Queen and is sentenced to death.

Memorable quote:

Lisa: Look! It's J.K. Rowling, author of the Harry Potter books! You've turned a generation of kids onto reading.

J.K. Rowling: Thank you, young Muggle.

Lisa: Can you tell me what happens at the end of the series?

J.K. Rowling: [*sigh*] He grows up and marries you. Is that what you want to hear?

Lisa: [*dreamily*] Yes.

And The President Wore Pearls (15)

After becoming class president, idealist Lisa is tricked into doing away with gym classes. If your bluffees are turned on by the music of Andrew Lloyd-Webber's *Evita*, then they'll be enchanted by 8-year-old Lisa Simpson belting out a parody of the world-famous musical's torch song *Rainbow High* from a balcony with her arms outstretched.

Memorable quote:

Police Chief Clancy Wiggum: Remember, these are little kids. So take out your *tiny* batons.

BOARD STUPID – THE WISDOM OF BART SIMPSON

At the beginning of most episodes – although it's often cut for time – Bart Simpson can be seen through the window of his schoolroom, in detention, writing lines on the blackboard.

One of the show's visual gags is that the message changes with each episode, often reflecting real events in the life of the show. Many people will react with almost spiritual awe if you can casually quote Bart's chalky atonements as if they were some sort of arcane Wisdom. Cracking examples include:

> *Tar is not a plaything*
> *I will not make flatulent noises in class*
> *Underwear should be worn on the inside*
> *I will not hide the teacher's Prozac*
> *Nobody likes sunburn slappers*
> *I will not fake rabies*
> *The principal's toupee is not a Frisbee*
> *I am not certified to remove asbestos*
> *Goldfish don't bounce*
> *I am not the reincarnation of Sammy Davis Jr.*
> *I will not send lard through the mail*
> *Nerve gas is not a toy*
> *I am not authorized to fire substitute teachers*
> *Pork is not a verb*
> *I will not bring sheep to class*
> *'Non-Flammable' is not a challenge*
> *I will not surprise the incontinent*

THE BRAINS OF THE OPERATION

The creative staff behind The Simpsons could fill a small telephone book. The team usually numbers around 25 writers, who sit around a table banging ideas back and forth until an embryonic draft storyline emerges.

The bluffer need not remember all past and current writers to successfully impress – indeed you could probably just make up a name and your audience, who by now will be hanging on every word, will swallow it hook, line and sinker. However, there have been some notable names over the years (aside from those already mentioned) that you might want to drop into conversation at whim, as well as the only non-American writer, Ricky Gervais:

Michael Carrington – Comedy writer and voice talent behind *The Simpsons'* one-off character Sideshow Raheem.

Dan Castellaneta – Voice talent for Homer Simpson; and his wife, **Deb Lacusta** – Writer

Greg Daniels – Comedy writer. It was he who adapted the BBC show *The Office* for American television.

Dana Gould – Writer and comedian.

Conan O'Brien – Talk-show host and writer.

Don Payne – Writer who worked on the movies *My Super Ex-Girlfriend* and *Fantastic Four: Rise of The Silver Surfer.*

Mike Scully – Co-writer and co-executive producer of *The Simpsons Movie.*

And it doesn't hurt to have a few soundbites about the Big Two up your sleeve:

Matt Groening

Matthew Abram Groening was born in Portland, Oregon, in 1954. He attended Evergreen State College (Evergreen Terrace link, anyone?) an establishment that he refers to as: "a hippie college, with no grades or required classes, that drew every creative weirdo in the Northwest."

For inspiration he says he drew upon "a combination of my own family and a lot of TV families and sitcoms that I grew up watching as a kid that have, sort of, mutated into the Simpsons."

Though the characters of Homer, Marge and Lisa are named after members of his family, he admits: "but I do have a brother and sister who I haven't humiliated by naming a Simpson after them and I can't tell who's more annoyed with me, the ones who were named – or the ones who weren't."

James L. Brooks

Jim Brooks is a veteran of television comedy, responsible for such iconic series as *The Mary Tyler Moore Show*, *Rhoda* (in which he starred as the unseen and lugubrious voice of Carlton, the Doorman), *Lou Grant* and *Taxi*. He also directed the movies *Terms of Endearment* and *As Good as It Gets* with Jack Nicholson and walked off with a string of Academy Awards.

At the end of each Simpsons' episode, there is a pictorial reference in the credits to Gracie Films. This is Jim Brooks' company. On the Simpsons annual *Treehouse of Horror* Halloween episodes, Brooks is credited as 'James Hell Brooks', 'Chains Hell Brooks', 'Maims Hell Brooks', 'Veins Hell Brooks', and 'James "Bemused But Bloodthirsty" Brooks'.

The rest of us just call him 'Lucky Jim'.

SAY WHAT?

So you can walk the walk as a bluffer, but can you talk the talk? We offer a quick run-down to *The Simpsons* most famous catchphrases for you to mimic.

D'oh! (annoyed grunt)   Stock response from Homer Simpson to illustrate angry frustration that only ever appears as "(annoyed grunt)" in the script. Both Lisa and Bart have inherited this phrase to a lesser extent. The "d'oh" sound is now so well-known that it has even made it into the *Oxford English Dictionary*.

Woo-hoo!   Homer's oft-used expression of delight. e.g:
"Mr Simpson, you've just won a year's supply of doughnuts and your father's emigrated."
"Woo-hoo!"

Why, you little...!   Homer's most angry expression. Always directed at Bart, always with Homer's hands tightly around Bart's neck.

Oh yeah!   Enthusiastic refrain of smooth-talking corporate promoter Duffman.

Eat my shorts!   Bart Simpson's most famed response and the one that caused the Establishment consider-able distress when it first appeared. Bart uses this insult, usually when speeding away from the recipient at a rate of knots.

¡Ay Caramba!   Another Bart speciality, although rarely uttered these days, apart from other characters – and *Simpsons* fans – trying to imitate Bart. Use to show shock or surprise.

Don't have a cow, man! Bart's version of 'Take it easy'. You could get away with saying it at the age of 10, but not much later. It is best to refrain from trying to construct permutations of any of these phrases. "Caramba – eat my cow, man!", for example, just sounds plain silly.

Hmmmmmm... Marge Simpson's trademark sound (given in the script only as 'frustrated murmur'). What it has come to signify is the all-encompassing response to any situation to which there is no adequate verbal retort. For a perfect frustrated Marge, try the following: clench your teeth together and then exhale heavily while at the same time adding a growl.

Yoinks! Oft-used expletive. Has evolved as a stock phrase for anyone in *The Simpsons* pinching something quickly and running away. Much favoured by Marge, Bart and Snake Jailbird.

Hee hee hee hee hee hee... Newcomers may be under the impression that Lisa Simpson doesn't have a catchphrase of her own. They're mistaken. She may not be very often in the right frame of mind, but when Lisa gets mischievous, she gives out this wicked little chuckle. If imitating, there should always be six 'Hee's.

Okly-diddly-doke (and variations on the theme) A thoroughly irritating catchphrase belonging to the Simpsons' neighbour Ned Flanders. In fact, he has dozens of them and they've even crept into the speech patterns of lesser mortals. Flanders feels the need to suffix almost every word with "-iddly" or "-doddly", or

"-doodly" or some other such gibberish. Bluffers should only adopt this habit if they are out of striking range of someone with a blunt instrument.

Eeeeeexcellent! Expostulation exclusively reserved for C. Montgomery Burns, Springfield's own 104-year-old megalomaniac. Is usually embellished with a sly wringing of the hands. May occasionally be followed by: "Release the hounds!"*

Ha-ha! Meaningless expression specific to Nelson Muntz, Springfield Elementary's bully. He has a finely honed sense of *schadenfreude* and will often be seen running into shot at the most inopportune – and unexpected – moments. For the musical bluffer, the first syllable is C# followed in quick succession by an F. Pick any old key, Nelson won't mind.

I'm Troy McClure. You may remember me from ... Until the tragic death of voice talent (Phil Hartman) in 1998, the character of Troy McClure popped up frequently in the show as a has-been actor continually introducing himself to his audience by way of his past successes – usually forgotten 'infomercials' and B-movies. For example: "I'm Troy McClure. You may remember me from such self-help tapes as 'Smoke yourself thin' and 'Get some confidence, Stupid!'

Hello, everybody! Salutation belonging to Springfield's favourite quack, Dr Nick Riviera. Should be spoken in a thick Mediterranean or Latino accent. Use this on your grand entrance and the assembled throng will be rolling around in the isles. Oh yeah.

* Burns' mansion is littered with these four-legged biting machines.

THE AUTHOR

There will undoubtedly be a few unkind souls who might ask if Paul Couch and Homer Simpson have ever been seen in the same room together. While it is true that there might be something of a superficial resemblance, the former knows some very good lawyers, so just watch it.

Couch (pronounced "Coosh", not "Cooch" or Cowch" has been a *Simpsons* über-bluffer ever since Matt Groening's first primitive sketches popped up on *The Tracey Ullman Show* in the 1980s. In his time, he has been a songwriter and broadcaster, written for the stage and television, edited newspapers and magazines, all with his one good eye on that elusive writing job in LA-LA Land (not Springfield – Hollywood).

He harbours no ill feeling towards Paramount Television over the fact that an unsolicited script for *Star Trek*, over which he had slaved for months, now sits in the bottom of a drawer because the franchise was axed within days of the work being completed. No, not one bit.

Paul Couch is married and resides in East Anglia. A trained actor, when suitably plied with alcohol his speciality impersonations include Homer, Marge, Moe, Mr Burns, Krusty the Clown, and his *pièce de résistance*, Dr Marvin Munroe. He lives in hope of one day providing voice talent for the show in lieu of not being involved in its scripts.

the Bluffer's® Guides

The five million-copy best-selling humour series that contains facts, jargon and inside information – all you need to know to hold your own among experts.

Accountancy

Astrology & Fortune Telling

Archaeology

James Bond

The Classics

Computers

Consultancy

Cricket

Divorce

Doctors

Economics

The Flight Deck

Football

Genetics

Golf

Jazz

Law

Management

Marketing

Men

Middle Age

Music

Opera

Paris

Philosophy

Psychology

Public Speaking

The Quantum Universe

Relationships

Rugby

Seduction

Sex

Skiing

Small Business

Stocks & Shares

Teaching

University

Whisky

Wine

Women

Available from all good bookshops, online, or direct from the publisher: in the UK (0)20 7193 1769 (post free), and in the USA 1-800-243-0495 (toll free). **www.bluffers.com**